HOW TO UPCYCLE NEARLY EVERYTHING

HOW TO UPCYCLE NEARLY EVERYTHING

CALIN DUKE

DUCHESS INK, 2023

ISBN 978-1-960367-00-6

How To Upcycle Nearly Everything
is dedicated to

Dora Dean Beesley

great grandmother,
great soul
and great upcycler.

Table of Contents

BUTTON UP SECTION

T-SHIRT SECTION

SWEATER SECTION

BIBLIOGRAPHY
ABOUT THE AUTHOR

WHAT EXACTLY <u>IS</u> UPCYCLING? WHY SHOULD YOU UPCYCLE?

So many questions, Dear Reader! First, 'upcycling' is just one of the many terms given to the process of reusing something and turning it into something else. Other terms you might see are: 'reusing,' 'recycling' and 'repurposing.' On the vocabulary page you will find a few terms that may help you on your upcycling journey.

Did you know that fast fashion is responsible for more carbon emissions than international travel and maritime shipping combined? Also, people all along the fashion supply chain (from cotton production to clothing disposal) are exploited to bring clothing to us at an ever-increasing rate. With this information in hand, it is easy to see why many feel despondent about the fashion industry. And while buying from sustainable companies can help, with over 92 million tons of clothing going into landfills worldwide every year, we can't just shop our way out of the problem! That's where this book comes in...

THE PROJECTS IN THIS BOOK SALVAGE ARTICLES OF CLOTHING THAT ARE OFTEN THROWN AWAY. INSTEAD, WE WILL BE USING THEM TO CREATE NEW (AND BETTER!) ITEMS. ONE OF THE WAYS YOU CAN PERSONALLY CHANGE THE FASHION WORLD IS TO UPCYCLE INSTEAD OF BUYING, WHENEVER POSSIBLE. IN ADDITION TO MAKING SOME OF THE PROJECTS IN THIS BOOK, I HOPE THAT THIS BOOK WILL SPARK YOUR IMAGINATION AND YOU COME UP WITH SOME OF YOUR OWN UPCYCLING IDEAS FOR STUFF THAT'S IN YOUR CLOSET!

PERSONALLY, I UPCYCLE INSTEAD OF BUYING NEW BECAUSE I GET TO:

⇒ DIVERT CLOTHING FROM LANDFILLS

⇒ CREATE CLOTHING AND HOUSEHOLD GOODS THAT ARE ONE-OF-A-KIND (NO ONE ELSE HAS A PILLOW QUITE LIKE MINE—PILLOW COVER, PAGE 4)

⇒ SAVE MONEY

⇒ HAVE A GREAT SENSE OF ACCOMPLISHMENT

I HOPE YOU ENJOY MAKING THESE PROJECTS AS MUCH AS I ENJOYED MAKING THIS BOOK FOR YOU!

VOCABULARY:

<u>FAST FASHION</u>: INEXPENSIVE CLOTHING PRODUCED RAPIDLY BY MASS-MARKET RETAILERS IN RESPONSE TO THE LATEST TRENDS. (OXFORD LANGUAGES ONLINE)

EX: "I'M NOT KOWTOWING TO FAST FASHION! I'M GONNA JUST MAKE A SKIRT FROM MY OLD T-SHIRTS RATHER THAN BUY A BRAND NEW ONE!" (PAGE 32)

<u>UPCYCLE</u>: THE PROCESS OF CONVERTING MATERIALS DESTINED FOR THE DUMP INTO PRODUCTS OF GREATER VALUE. (URBAN DICTIONARY)

EX: "CHECK OUT THIS COOL STOCKING CAP THAT I UPCYCLED FROM AN OLD SWEATER!" (PAGE 38)

<u>REPURPOSE</u>: TO USE SOMETHING FOR A DIFFERENT PURPOSE FOR WHICH IT WAS INTENDED. (CAMBRIDGE ENGLISH DICTIONARY)

EX: "I REPURPOSED THIS JAM JAR INTO A CONTAINER TO HOLD ALL MY BUTTONS."

REUSE: TO USE AGAIN OR MORE THAN ONCE. (OXFORD LANGUAGE DICTIONARY)

EX: "I'LL REUSE THESE STRAPS FROM AN OLD TOTE ON THE NEW ONE THAT I'M MAKING FROM AN UPCYCLED BUTTON-UP." (PAGE 8)

RECYCLE: TO BREAK DOWN WHAT'S ALREADY BEEN USED AND MAKE IT INTO SOMETHING ELSE THAT APPEARS BRAND NEW. (URBAN DICTIONARY)

EX: "IF I ABSOLUTELY CAN NOT MEND, REPAIR, REUSE OR UPCYCLE SOMETHING THEN I RECYCLE IT!"

MEND/REPAIR: TO FIX SOMETHING SO YOU CAN CONTINUE TO USE IT AS INTENDED. (CALIN DUKE ☺)

EX: "I'M GONNA MEND THE @$#% OUT OF MY SWEATER BY COVERING ALL THE MOTH HOLES WITH CUTE PINK HEART PATCHES!"

SEWING TERMS USED IN THIS BOOK:

Okay, so now you feel a bit more savvy with your arsenal of words. You can officially hang out at a hipster barbeque without embarrassing yourself. Expand your lexicon further with these sewing terms to gain bonus social points AND (more importantly) be able to complete any of the projects in this book. Also, in this book I am assuming that you have some basic sewing skills.

RIGHT SIDE (OF THE FABRIC): The side of the fabric intended to be seen. Think of a bright cotton print or fake fur and the "right side" becomes pretty obvious.

WRONG SIDE (OF THE FABRIC): The side of the fabric NOT intended to be seen (although, such a judgey name, no?).

SEAM: The stitching holding two (or more) pieces of fabric together. You often see seams on the sides of garments.

SEAM ALLOWANCE: Extra amount of fabric used to create the seam.

HEM: The finished off edge of a garment, oftentimes created by folding fabric over itself.
NOTE: I used to get 'seam' and 'hem' confused for an embarrassingly long time. Give yourself a mnemonic device that works for you (e.g: "seams like there are two pieces of fabric held together here!").

HEM →

TACK: To hold fabric in place or several pieces of fabric together by making one or two stitches by hand. For example, you might fold over a pant cuff and tack it down at the side seams to hold it in place.

SEWING SUPPLIES: Unless otherwise indicated, this means: scissors, pins, and either a sewing machine or thread and needle.

BASTING: To hold fabric in place with long loose stitches (usually done by hand) before sewing down for good. Basting holds fabric in place more substantially than pinning and is often done with slippery or hard-to-manage fabric at a hem or seam.

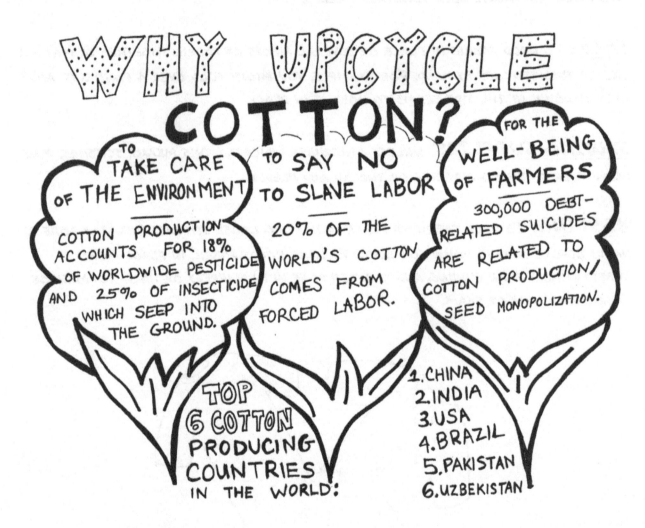

PILLOW COVER

- **A BUTTON UP**

    —ALOHA SHIRTS WORK GREAT!

- **PILLOW FORM/PILLOW**

    —PERHAPS YOU ALREADY HAVE AN UGLY PILLOW THAT YOU WANT TO COVER?

- **MEASURING DEVICE**

    —SUCH AS RULER OR MEASURING TAPE

- **SEWING SUPPLIES**

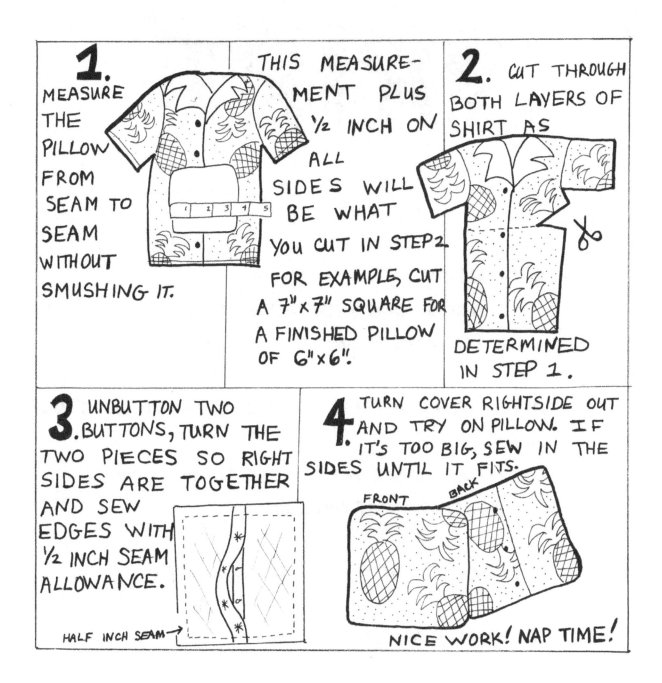

1. MEASURE THE PILLOW FROM SEAM TO SEAM WITHOUT SMUSHING IT.

THIS MEASURE-MENT PLUS ½ INCH ON ALL SIDES WILL BE WHAT YOU CUT IN STEP 2. FOR EXAMPLE, CUT A 7" x 7" SQUARE FOR A FINISHED PILLOW OF 6" x 6".

2. CUT THROUGH BOTH LAYERS OF SHIRT AS DETERMINED IN STEP 1.

3. UNBUTTON TWO BUTTONS, TURN THE TWO PIECES SO RIGHT SIDES ARE TOGETHER AND SEW EDGES WITH ½ INCH SEAM ALLOWANCE.

HALF INCH SEAM →

4. TURN COVER RIGHTSIDE OUT AND TRY ON PILLOW. IF IT'S TOO BIG, SEW IN THE SIDES UNTIL IT FITS.

FRONT   BACK

NICE WORK! NAP TIME!

- **A T-SHIRT**
  - -CHOOSE ONE WITH INTERESTING GRAPHICS/DESIGN

- **A BUTTON-UP THAT FITS OVER YOUR HIPS AND BUM**
  - -THE LOOSER THE FIT, THE ROOMIER THE FINISHED SKIRT WILL BE

- **A PLACE TO GET PARTIALLY NAKED**

- **SEWING SUPPLIES**

1 FROM THE T-SHIRT, CUT A STRIP OFF THE BOTTOM ROUGHLY TWICE THE WIDTH YOU WANT THE WAISTBAND TO BE.

2 FOLD STRIP IN HALF ON ITSELF TO FORM A WAISTBAND.

3 FIT THE WAIST-BAND BY TRYING IT ON. IF IT'S TOO LARGE, OPEN IT UP AND TAKE IT IN.

IF YOU'RE FEELING DARING, TAKE IT IN LIKE SO TO CREATE A TAPERED WAISTBAND.

4 CUT THE BUTTON-UP BELOW THE ARMPIT. IF NEEDED, TRIM FROM THE RAW EDGE TO MAKE THE FINISHED SKIRT THE LENGTH YOU WANT IT.

5 PLACE FOLDED WAISTBAND -RAW EDGES TO RAW EDGES- AROUND THE BUTTON-UP. PIN IN PLACE AND SEW, STRETCHING WAISTBAND TO FIT BUTTON-UP.

SEW HERE

6 FLIP THE WAISTBAND UP AND ENJOY YOUR SKIRT!

UNBUTTON AS PER YOUR MOOD.

TOTE BAG

- **A BUTTON-UP**
  - TWO IF YOUR BAG IS GOING TO BE LINED

- **TWO STRAPS, APPROX. 32 INCHES LONG**
GET CREATIVE HERE! YOU CAN USE:
  ⇒ WEBBING (ONE TO TWO INCHES WIDE)
  ⇒ BELTS
  ⇒ STRAPS FROM ANOTHER TOTE
  ⇒ NECKTIES

- **SEWING SUPPLIES**

1 CUT THE BUTTON UP JUST BELOW THE SLEEVES.

2 NOW, DECIDE IF YOUR TOTE WILL BE THIS WAY (and you can use the pockets).

OR

THIS WAY (and you can use finished hem for the top of tote).

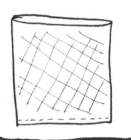

3 TURN INSIDE-OUT, RIGHT SIDES TOGETHER AND SEW THE BOTTOM OF YOUR TOTE.

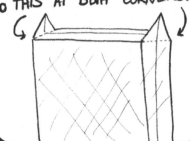

4 LINE UP THE SEAM YOU JUST MADE AND THE SHIRT SIDE, MAKING A TRIANGLE. SEW ACROSS THE WIDTH YOU WANT YOUR TOTE TO BE. DO THIS AT BOTH CORNERS.

5 (if you chose to use finished hem for the top, skip this step)
TURN THE RIGHT SIDE OVER 1/4 INCH, PRESS AND REPEAT. SEW DOWN AROUND OPENING. NOW FOR THE STRAPS...

3 STRAP IDEAS

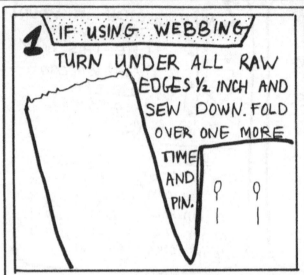

1 IF USING WEBBING
TURN UNDER ALL RAW EDGES ½ INCH AND SEW DOWN. FOLD OVER ONE MORE TIME AND PIN.

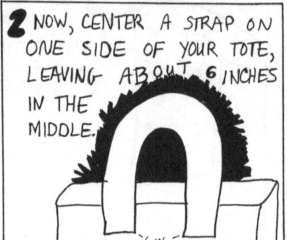

2 NOW, CENTER A STRAP ON ONE SIDE OF YOUR TOTE, LEAVING ABOUT 6 INCHES IN THE MIDDLE.

~6 IN.~

WEBBING

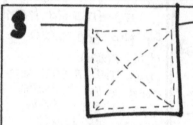

3 PIN ENDS IN PLACE AND SEW AS INDICATED ABOVE.

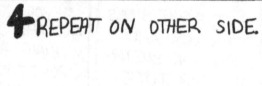

4 REPEAT ON OTHER SIDE.

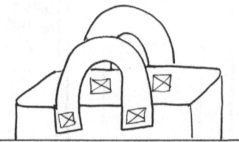

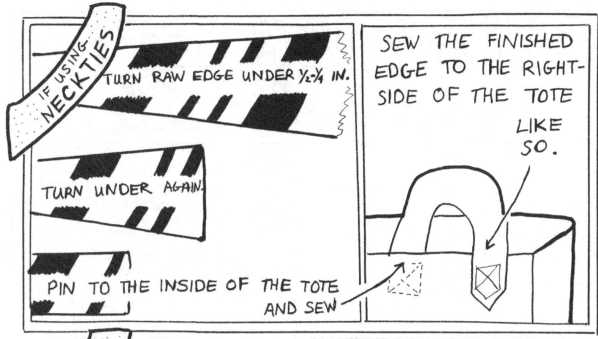

CUSTOMIZE IT!

Reversible Tote

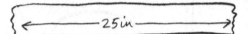
25 in

1 CUT TWO PIECES FROM YOUR STRAP MATERIAL TO ABOUT 25 INCHES EACH (OR WHATEVER LENGTH SITS WELL FOR YOU + 1" SEAM ALLOWANCE PER STRAP).

SHIRT A

SHIRT B

2 NOW, WITH EACH OF YOUR SHIRTS, DO STEPS 1-4 OF MAKING A TOTE FROM A BUTTON-UP SHIRT.

3 PIN A STRAP, CENTERED, TO THE FRONT OF SHIRT B TOTE, LEAVING ABOUT 6" BETWEEN THE STRAPS INNER EDGES. DO THE SAME ON TOTE BACK.

THIS SIDE, TOO
6 in
SHIRT B

4 SECURE STRAPS TO TOTE AT ALL FOUR POINTS BY SEWING BACK AND FORTH SEVERAL TIMES.

5 UNBUTTON 2 BUTTONS OF SHIRT A TOTE.

6 TURN SHIRT A TOTE INSIDE-OUT.

← SHIRT B TOTE

← SHIRT A TOTE

7 PUT SHIRT B TOTE INSIDE OF SHIRT A TOTE.

8 PIN TOGETHER AT TOP EDGE AND SEW ALL THE WAY AROUND WITH 1/2" SEAM ALLOWANCE, TURN RIGHT-SIDE OUT THROUGH OPENING, BUTTON AND...

TOTES FAB!

DRAWSTRING BAG

- **A BUTTON UP**
    - -WITH A HEM THAT YOU CAN CUT TWO IDENTICAL PIECES FROM

- **RIBBON, SHOELACE OR T-SHIRT ROPE** (PAGE 28)

- **SEWING SUPPLIES**

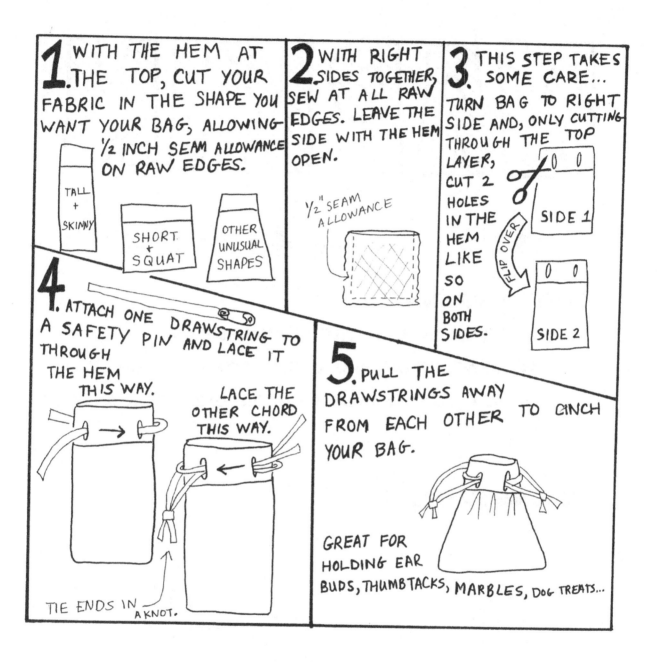

1. WITH THE HEM AT THE TOP, CUT YOUR FABRIC IN THE SHAPE YOU WANT YOUR BAG, ALLOWING ½ INCH SEAM ALLOWANCE ON RAW EDGES.

TALL + SKINNY

SHORT + SQUAT

OTHER UNUSUAL SHAPES

2. WITH RIGHT SIDES TOGETHER, SEW AT ALL RAW EDGES. LEAVE THE SIDE WITH THE HEM OPEN.

½" SEAM ALLOWANCE

3. THIS STEP TAKES SOME CARE... TURN BAG TO RIGHT SIDE AND, ONLY CUTTING THROUGH THE TOP LAYER, CUT 2 HOLES IN THE HEM LIKE SO ON BOTH SIDES.

FLIP OVER

SIDE 1

SIDE 2

4. ATTACH ONE DRAWSTRING TO A SAFETY PIN AND LACE IT THROUGH THE HEM THIS WAY.

LACE THE OTHER CHORD THIS WAY.

TIE ENDS IN A KNOT.

5. PULL THE DRAWSTRINGS AWAY FROM EACH OTHER TO CINCH YOUR BAG.

GREAT FOR HOLDING EAR BUDS, THUMBTACKS, MARBLES, DOG TREATS...

NAPKIN

- BUTTON-UP SHIRT OR
    ⇒ JUST THE BACK OF THE BUTTON-UP OR...
    ⇒ ANY FLAT BIT OF FABRIC SCRAP BIG ENOUGH FOR
       THESE PROJECTS SUCH AS A PILLOWCASE, A SHEET,
       ETC.

- SEWING SUPPLIES

1.

CUT A SQUARE PIECE OUT OF YOUR GARMENT. THE SQUARE SHOULD BE 1 INCH BIGGER THAN YOU WANT YOUR FINISHED NAPKIN TO BE. FOR EXAMPLE, CUT A 17"x 17" SQUARE FOR A FINISHED NAPKIN THAT IS 16"x16".

2.

ON OPPOSITE SIDES OF YOUR SQUARE, FOLD OVER ¼" AND IRON FLAT.

FOLD OVER AGAIN AND IRON AGAIN.

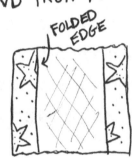

3.

REPEAT THIS PROCESS ON THE REMAINING SIDES OF YOUR SQUARE.

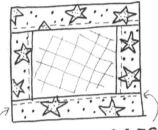

SEW ALL EDGES DOWN.

BEHOLD, A NAPKIN!

CAN BE SO MANY THINGS...

NOW THAT YOU'VE MADE A NAPKIN (A SQUARE PIECE OF FABRIC!!) YOU HAVE THE SKILLS TO MAKE MANY OTHER THINGS- WITH A FEW MINOR MODIFICATIONS. I HAVE SHARED A FEW OF THESE IDEAS ON THE FOLLOWING PAGES. REMEMBER, TO HAVE FINISHED DIMENSIONS AS GIVEN BELOW, YOU WILL NEED TO START WITH A PIECE OF FABRIC THAT IS AN INCH BIGGER ALL AROUND (E.G.: FOR A FINISHED SQUARE OF 12"X12" YOU NEED TO START WITH A 13"X13" PIECE OF FABRIC).

SCARVES: FOR A FASHIONABLE SCARF, USE VERY LIGHT COTTON OR EVEN SILK (UPCYCLED BUTTON-UPS, BED SHEETS, DRESSES, SKIRTS). THERE ARE SO MANY DIFFERENT DIMENSIONS YOU CAN MAKE BUT SOME EXAMPLES OF COMMON FINISHED DIMENSIONS ARE 27.5" X 27.5" OR 21" X 21" AND, FOR A LONG RECTANGULAR SCARF, 8" X 60" IS A GOOD PLACE TO START.

TIP: I WOULD RECOMMEND IRONING DOWN THE HEMS ON THE EDGES (AND/OR BASTING) BEFORE MACHINE STITCHING AS BOTH SILK AND LIGHT COTTON CAN BE SLIPPERY.

BANDANA: USE LIGHTWEIGHT COTTON (UPCYCLED BUTTON UP, BEDSHEET, DRESS, ETC.). FINISHED BANDANA DIMENSIONS ARE USUALLY 12" X 12". MY FAVORITE WAY TO WEAR MY BANDANA WHEN I'M IN THE GARDEN, ON A HIKE OR DOING OTHER "SERIOUS WORK/SERIOUS PLAY:"

FOLD BANDANA IN HALF LIKE SO.

PLACE ON YOUR HEAD WITH THE LONG FLAT EDGE ON YOUR FOREHEAD AND THE TRIANGLE POINT IN BACK. HOLD THE OTHER ENDS OF THE TRIANGLE IN YOUR HAND AND...

TIE TOGETHER IN BACK LIKE SO.

ENJOY LOOKING CUTE AND NO SWEAT ON YOUR BROW AS YOU FROLIC.

WRAPPING CLOTH: FUROSHIKI IS THE NAME OF TRADITIONAL JAPANESE WRAPPING CLOTH AND IT IS AN **AWESOME** SUSTAINABLE ALTERNATIVE TO WRAPPING PAPER. USE LIGHT COTTON OR REALLY ANYTHING THAT IS PRETTY (UPCYCLED BUTTON UPS, BED SHEETS, DRESSES, AND SKIRTS). FUROSHIKI IS ALSO A FABULOUS WAY TO USE UP FABRIC SCRAPS OR OLD SILK SCARVES. A FINISHED DIMENSION OF 19.5" X 19.5" IS A GOOD SIZE FOR WRAPPING A BOOK.

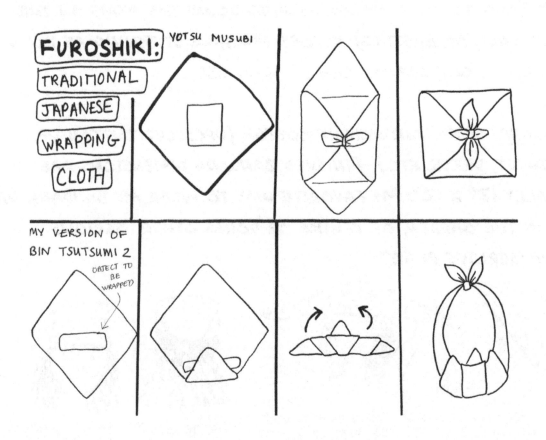

TIP: You can make your wrapping cloth double sided; this way both sides are decorative when shown. If you do choose to make it double-sided, just consider the thickness and how it will handle being tied. Also, there are a multitude of resources online to learn about different wrapping techniques for different shaped gifts.

Place Mat: Use heavy weight cotton that is washable (upcycled curtains, denim). Finished dimensions are often 12" x 18". For a little variety in your dining experiences, sew together two DIFFERENT color heavy fabrics as shown below and have double sided place mats.

CUT TWO RECTANGULAR PIECES. I RECOMMEND TWO 13" x 19" PIECES FOR A PLACEMAT OF 12" x 18".

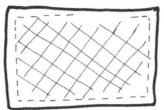

SEW THE TWO PIECES RIGHT SIDES TOGETHER, LEAVING SPACE TO TURN RIGHTSIDE OUT.

TURN RIGHTSIDE OUT THROUGH OPENING, USE SHARP OBJECT TO PUSH CORNERS OUT AND HANDSTITCH THE OPENING SHUT.

- **A COLORFUL BUTTON-UP**
  - OR SCRAPS FROM BUTTON-UPS, PERHAPS FROM OTHER FABULOUS PROJECTS?

- **7 INCHES OF ¼" ELASTIC**

- **LARGE SAFETY PIN**

- **SEWING SUPPLIES**
  - INCLUDING THREAD AND SEWING NEEDLE

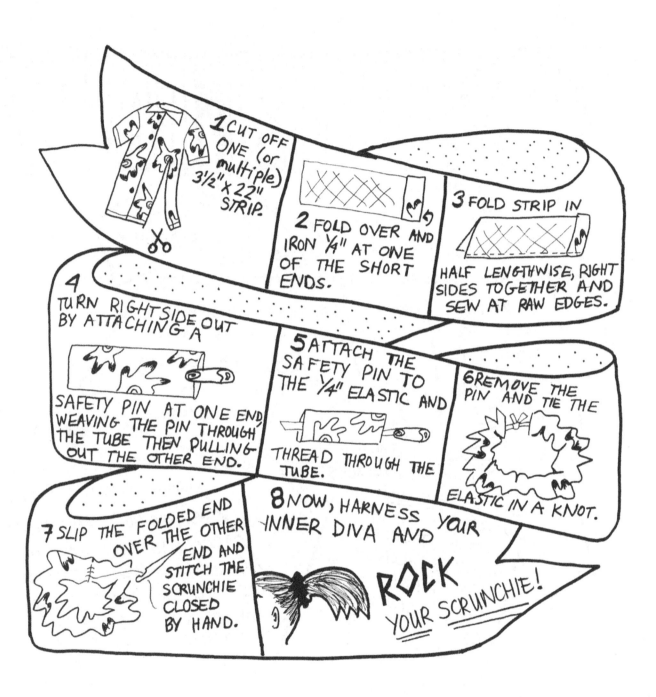

1 CUT OFF ONE (or multiple) 3½" X 22" STRIP.

2 FOLD OVER AND IRON ¼" AT ONE OF THE SHORT ENDS.

3 FOLD STRIP IN HALF LENGTHWISE, RIGHT SIDES TOGETHER AND SEW AT RAW EDGES.

4 TURN RIGHTSIDE OUT BY ATTACHING A SAFETY PIN AT ONE END, WEAVING THE PIN THROUGH THE TUBE THEN PULLING OUT THE OTHER END.

5 ATTACH THE SAFETY PIN TO THE ¼" ELASTIC AND THREAD THROUGH THE TUBE.

6 REMOVE THE PIN AND TIE THE ELASTIC IN A KNOT.

7 SLIP THE FOLDED END OVER THE OTHER END AND STITCH THE SCRUNCHIE CLOSED BY HAND.

8 NOW, HARNESS YOUR INNER DIVA AND ROCK YOUR SCRUNCHIE!

- **MULTIPLE T-SHIRTS**
  - OLD ONES! DO **NOT** BUY NEW ONES! RAID YOUR CLOSET, RAID THE CLOSET OF A LOVED ONE, GO TO THE THRIFT!

- **A GLASS QUART JAR WITH A PLASTIC LID**

- **RUBBING ALCOHOL**

- **DISH SOAP**

- **WARM WATER**

1 CUT YOUR T-SHIRT INTO GOOD-SIZED SQUARES. THEY CAN BE WHATEVER SIZE FEELS GOOD IN YOUR HANDS. TRY 8"X8" TO START AND GO FROM THERE.

2 MIX TOGETHER:

- 2 CUPS OF WARM WATER
- 1 TABLESPOON DISH SOAP
- 1 CUP RUBBING ALCOHOL (70% OR HIGHER)

  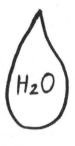

3 PLACE THE T-SHIRT SQUARES AND MIXTURE FROM STEP 2 IN A HEATPROOF JAR WITH A NON-METAL LID.

4 TO USE "WET WIPES":

- TAKE OUT ONE WIPE AT A TIME, WRINGING EXCESS LIQUID INTO JAR
- CLEAN SOME STUFF (YOUR HANDS, TABLETOP, YOUR KID...)
- RETURN WIPE TO JAR (IF LIGHTLY USED) OR PUT SOILED WIPE IN WITH YOUR LAUNDRY.

T-SHIRT ROPE

CROCHET RUG (or pot holder)

HOODIE DRAWSTRING

LACING CORSETS + BOOTS

AS A RIBBON SUBSTITUTE WITH FLOWERS + GIFTS

SOME IDEAS FOR T-SHIRT ROPE

LACING LEATHER POUCHES

MACRAME PLANT HANGERS

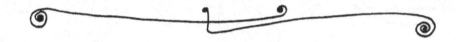

- 8 (OR ANY EVEN NUMBER OF ROPE) CUT INTO PIECES THAT ARE 3-4 FEET LONG

- A POT (WITH OR WITHOUT A PLANT)

1 CUT AN EVEN NUMBER (8 IS GOOD) OF T-SHIRT ROPE to TWO TIMES THE LENGTH YOU WANT YOUR FINISHED HANGER TO BE.

2 TIE THEM ALL IN ONE BIG KNOT.....

3 MAKE KNOTS IN PAIRS OF ROPES LIKE SO...

4
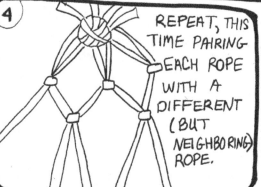
REPEAT, THIS TIME PAIRING EACH ROPE WITH A DIFFERENT (BUT NEIGHBORING) ROPE.

5
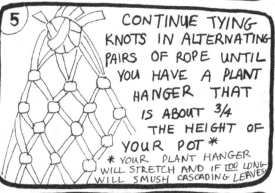
CONTINUE TYING KNOTS IN ALTERNATING PAIRS OF ROPE UNTIL YOU HAVE A PLANT HANGER THAT IS ABOUT 3/4 THE HEIGHT OF YOUR POT *
* YOUR PLANT HANGER WILL STRETCH AND IF TOO LONG WILL SMUSH CASCADING LEAVES

6 PLACE POT (AND/OR PLANT) INSIDE THE PLANT HANGER, STRETCHING AND REARRANGING ROPE TO MAKE PRETTY.

7 TIE ALL THE ROPES TOGETHER IN ONE KNOT, HANG FROM THE KNOT AND TELL ALL WHO LOOK UPON YOUR PLANT HANGER: "I MADE THAT!"

T-SHIRT-SKIRT

FROM TWO T-SHIRTS

- **2 UNUSUAL T-SHIRTS**
    - —YOUR SIZE OR LARGER

- **A PLACE TO GET PARTIALLY NAKED**

- **SEWING SUPPLIES**

STRETCHY GROCERY TOTE

- ## AN UNUSUAL T-SHIRT

- ## SEWING SUPPLIES

1 TURN YOUR T-SHIRT INSIDE OUT.

LINE UP THE BOTTOM EDGES.

2 SEW THROUGH FRONT AND BACK OF T-SHIRT ABOUT 1 INCH FROM BOTTOM HEM.

APPX. 1 INCH

3 TURN RIGHTSIDE OUT.

YAY! UNICORNS!

4 LOOK, A UNICORN!

CUT THE SLEEVES OFF TO MAKE HANDLES (NO NEED TO CUT THESE VERY DEEP AS THEY WILL STRETCH OVER TIME).

5 ME ENCANTAN LOS UNICORNIOS!

CUT OFF THE T-SHIRT NECK (THROUGH BOTH SIDES).

6 GENTLY STRETCH THE HANDLES AND START USING YOUR TOTE!

I ♥ UNICORNS!

SOME SWEATER FIBER FACTS

ALPACA	CASHMERE	WOOL

ALPACA
- ALPACA CUT GRASS (RATHER THAN PULL IT UP BY THE ROOTS)
- ALPACAS' SOFT FEET DON'T DESTROY THE EARTH
- ONE ADULT PRODUCES ENOUGH FIBER IN A YEAR TO MAKE 4 SWEATERS
- BUYING ALPACA OFTEN SUPPORTS INDIGENUOUS COMMUNITIES

CASHMERE
- GOATS PULL UP GRASS BY THE ROOTS, LEADING TO DESERTIFICATION
- GOAT HOOVES ALSO DESTROY THE SOIL
- IT TAKES 4 YEARS FOR A GOAT TO GROW ENOUGH HAIR TO PRODUCE 1 SWEATER

WOOL

- SHEEP GRAZING HAS LED TO DESERTIFICATION
- EASILY RECYCLED
- WHEN BLENDED WITH SYNTHETICS (WHICH IS OFTEN) IT CONTRIBUTES TO MICROPLASTICS (AKA: TINY PLASTICS FOUND IN THE OCEAN AND ELSEWHERE)
- STAYS WARM WHEN WET

STOCKING CAP

- **THE TORSO PART OF A SWEATER**
    - ⇒ 2 sweaters (or one VERY LARGE sweater) if making a custom cap (PAGE 40)
    - ⇒ Save the sleeves for boots socks (PAGE 44) and/or fingerless gloves (PAGE 42)

- **A CAP THAT FITS WELL**
    - —TO BE USED AS A PATTERN, NOT DESTROYED

- **SEWING SUPPLIES**

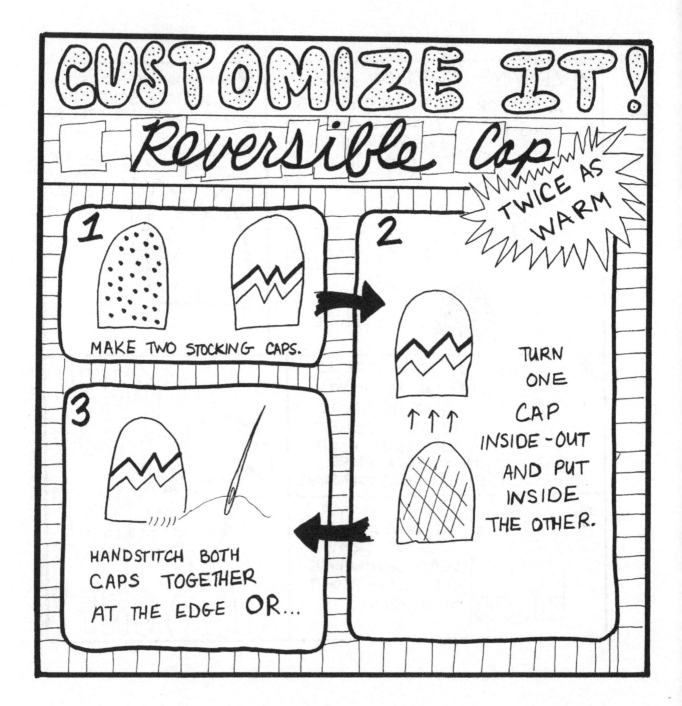

4 SEW ALONG THE EDGE.

WITH A SEWING-MACHINE, STITCH THE TWO RIGHT SIDES TOGETHER, LEAVING A SMALL GAP.

PUSH BOTH CAPS THROUGH THE GAP, TURNING THEM TO RIGHT SIDES. STITCH UP THE SMALL OPENING BY HAND... OR

5 TO CREATE A CAP WITH A CONTRASTING RIM ON ONE SIDE, MAKE ONE CAP SLIGHTLY LONGER THAN THE OTHER (ABOUT 2 IN.), PLACE IT INSIDE THE SMALLER CAP, FLIP UP EXCESS AND TACK DOWN AT SIDE SEAMS.

6 I doff my cap to you!

(LATER, I'LL DOFF IT LATER. NOW IT'S KEEPING MY HEAD REALLY WARM!)

Fingerless Gloves

- **BOTH SLEEVES OF A SWEATER**
  - —CASHMERE, MERINO WOOL OR OTHER THIN MATERIALS WORK BEST

- **SEWING SUPPLIES**

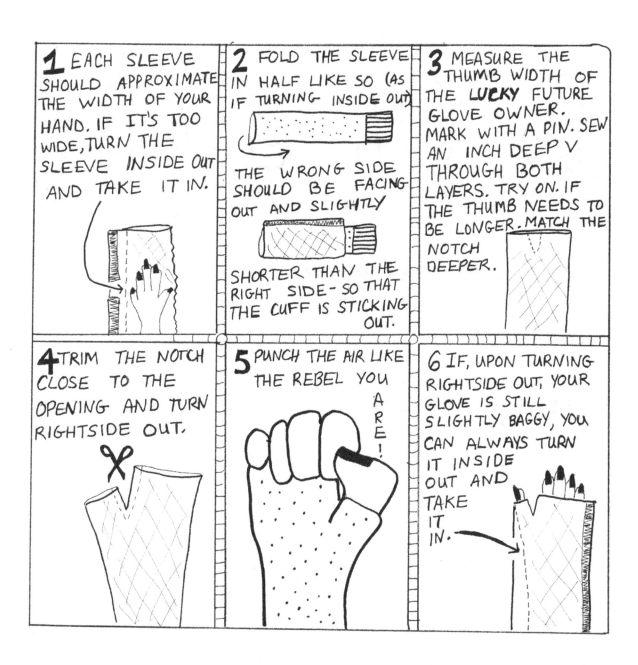

1 EACH SLEEVE SHOULD APPROXIMATE THE WIDTH OF YOUR HAND. IF IT'S TOO WIDE, TURN THE SLEEVE INSIDE OUT AND TAKE IT IN.

2 FOLD THE SLEEVE IN HALF LIKE SO (AS IF TURNING INSIDE OUT)

THE WRONG SIDE SHOULD BE FACING OUT AND SLIGHTLY

SHORTER THAN THE RIGHT SIDE - SO THAT THE CUFF IS STICKING OUT.

3 MEASURE THE THUMB WIDTH OF THE **LUCKY** FUTURE GLOVE OWNER. MARK WITH A PIN. SEW AN INCH DEEP V THROUGH BOTH LAYERS. TRY ON. IF THE THUMB NEEDS TO BE LONGER. MATCH THE NOTCH DEEPER.

4 TRIM THE NOTCH CLOSE TO THE OPENING AND TURN RIGHTSIDE OUT.

5 PUNCH THE AIR LIKE THE REBEL YOU ARE!

6 IF, UPON TURNING RIGHTSIDE OUT, YOUR GLOVE IS STILL SLIGHTLY BAGGY, YOU CAN ALWAYS TURN IT INSIDE OUT AND TAKE IT IN.

BOOT SOCKS

- BOTH SLEEVES OF A SWEATER

- HEAVY SOCKS

- SEWING SUPPLIES

1 MAKE SURE YOUR SOCKS ARE CLEAN AND RIGHT SIDE OUT.

2 IF THE SLEEVES OF THE SWEATER ARE NOT STRAIGHT, TURN INSIDE OUT AND SEW THEM STRAIGHT. KEEP INSIDE OUT.

3 TAKE ONE INSIDE-OUT SLEEVE AND PUT RIGHTSIDE-OUT SOCK INSIDE OF IT. LINING THE TOP OF THE SOCK WITH THE SLEEVE'S RAW EDGE, SEW AROUND THE SOCK WITH ½" SEAM ALLOWANCE. REPEAT PROCESS TO CREATE BOOT SOCK NUMBER TWO. TURN RIGHTSIDE-OUT AND...

½ INCH SEAM ALLOWANCE

ROCK OUT WITH YOUR SOCKS OUT!

BIBLIOGRAPHY

INTRODUCTION

Fashion's Carbon Emissions: McFall-Johnsen, Morgan. "The Fashion Industry Emits More Carbon than International Flights and Maritime Shipping Combined. Here Are the Biggest Ways It Impacts the Planet." *Business Insider*, Business Insider, 21 Oct. 2019, https://www.businessinsider.com/fast-fashion-environmental-impact-pollution-emissions-waste-water-2019-10#in-total-up-to-85-of-textiles-go-into-landfills-each-year-thats-enough-to-fill-the-sydney-harbor-annually-6.

92 Million Tons of Waste Annually: Mulhern, Owen. "The 10 Essential Fast Fashion Statistics." *Earth.Org*, 28 July 2022, earth.org/fast-fashion-statistics/.

PAGE 2 *COTTON*

Environment: "Environmental Impact." *The True Cost*, https://truecostmovie.com/learn-more/environmental-impact/.

Slave Labor: John Sudworth. "China's 'Tainted' Cotton." *BBC News*, BBC, 2021, https://www.bbc.co.uk/news/extra/nz0g306v8c/china-tainted-cotton.

Farmers: Thomas, Gigesh, and Johan De Tavernier. "Farmer-Suicide in India: Debating the Role of Biotechnology." *Life Sciences, Society and Policy*, Springer Berlin Heidelberg, Dec. 2017, https://www.ncbi.nlm.nih.gov/pmc/articles/PMC5427059/.

Top 6 Cotton Producing Countries: Shahbandeh, M. "World Cotton Production by Country 2019." *Statista*, 24 Aug. 2021, https://www.statista.com/statistics/263055/cotton-production-worldwide-by-top-countries/.

PAGE 21 *FUROSHIKI*

About: Kondo, Marie. "Furoshiki: Japanese Gift Wrapping – Konmari: The Official Website of Marie Kondo." *KonMari*, 4 Nov. 2021, https://konmari.com/furoshiki/.

How To: Gregory, Anna. "How to: Furoshiki (Japanese Fabric Wrapping)." 1 Million Women, 22 Nov. 2016, https://www.1millionwomen.com.au/blog/how-furoshiki-fabric-wrapping/.

PAGE 24 *T-SHIRTS*

Fact 1: Pero, Kel. "The Carbon Footprint of a T-Shirt." *Fairware Promotional Products*, 3 Oct. 2018, https://fairware.com/the-carbon-footprint-of-a-t-shirt/.

Facts 2, 3 and 4: TEDEducation. "The Life Cycle of a T-Shirt - Angel Chang." *YouTube*, YouTube, 5 Sept. 2017, https://www.youtube.com/watch?app=desktop&v=BiSYoeqb_VY&t=360s.

Additional Information: "The Impact of a Cotton T-Shirt." *WWF*, World Wildlife Fund, 16 Jan. 2013, https://www.worldwildlife.org/stories/the-impact-of-a-cotton-t-shirt.

PAGE 36 *SWEATER/DIFFERENT FIBERS*

Alpaca: Saville, Ellen. "3 Reasons Why Alpaca Is the Greenest Fibre on Earth." *Sustainable Publication For Eco Brands And Conscious People.*, 30 Aug. 2021, https://mochni.com/3-reasons-why-alpaca-is-the-greenest-fibre-on-earth/.

Breyer, Melissa. "8 Fun Facts about Alpacas." *Treehugger*, Treehugger, 19 Dec. 2020, https://www.treehugger.com/things-you-didnt-know-about-alpacas-4864274.

Cashmere: "Sustainable Fabrics • Guide on the Most Ethical Materials [2020]." *SustainYourStyle*, https://www.sustainyourstyle.org/en/fiber-ecoreview.

Wool: "Merino vs Alpaca: Comparing Natural Fibers." *Appalachian Gear Company*, https://appalachiangearcompany.com/blogs/appgear-insider/merino-vs-alpaca-comparing-natural-fibers.

ABOUT THE AUTHOR

CALIN DUKE IS AN AUTHOR, STORYTELLER AND UPCYCLER. IN ADDITION TO BEING A WORKING COSTUME DESIGNER, SHE WAS ONE OF THE COFOUNDERS OF THE KOHALA TRASH BASH FASHION SHOW IN 2006 IN HAWI, HAWAI'I AND HAS STUDIED FASHION AND STREETWEAR DESIGN AT PARSONS SCHOOL OF DESIGN. AMONG THE MANY THINGS SHE HAS WRITTEN ARE HER TWO BOOKS <u>HOW TO UPCYCLE NEARLY EVERYTHING</u> AND <u>A NANTUCKET PLATEFUL</u>--THE OFFICIAL CHILDREN'S BOOK FOR NANTUCKET PUBLIC SCHOOL'S NUTRITION PROGRAM.

ADDITIONALLY, CALIN IS A STORYTELLER, AND SHE REGULARLY PERFORMS HER ORIGINAL WORK BEFORE A LIVE AUDIENCE. SHE CURRENTLY LIVES IN MASSACHUSETTS WHERE SHE LIKES TO SPEND AS MUCH TIME AS POSSIBLE WITH HER PARTNER AND TWO BIG DOGS PLAYING IN THE WOODS.

CAN YOU DO ME A SOLID?

Write a FIVE STAR review for this book on AMAZON.

Check out and like my videos on YouTube @CalinDuke

The next time you want to go shopping, look in your closet first and see if you have anything there that will make do instead.

Try to NOT BUY ANY NEW CLOTHES for 2 months. Instead:
- Shop your closet
- Borrow from friends
- Look for free boxes, giveaways or buy nothing communities
- Shop at local thrift stores or used clothing sites online.

Thank you! Your support means the world to me.

ALL BOOKS—EVEN SMALLISH ONES LIKE THIS ONE—TAKE AN ENORMOUS AMOUNT OF WORK AND SUPPORT FROM A TEAM.

ENORMOUS THANK YOUS TO:

MY MOTHER, JUDY DUKE, FOR INTRODUCING ME TO THRIFT STORES, SEWING AND THE SATISFACTION OF RESOURCEFULNESS.

MY SISTER, JENNIE DUKE... FOR EVERYTHING. ♥

EMMA YOUNG FOR SHOWING ME HOW TO DO THE SERIOUS WORK OF UPCYCLING WITH A LOT OF HUMOR..

TOM STODDART FOR TELLING ME NOT TO TAKE ART CLASSES BECAUSE IT WOULD RUIN MY STYLE.

LOIS GERSON, HARRIET STICH, ANDY STICH, ERIC STICH AND MICHELLE WHELAN FOR REVIEWING MY WORK AND GIVING ME HONEST FEEDBACK.

BEN STICH FOR YOUR UNFLAGGING INSISTENCE ON EXCELLENCE IN THE MAKING OF THIS BOOK AND IN EVERYTHING YOU DO. THIS BOOK WOULD NOT HAVE BEEN POSSIBLE WITHOUT YOU.

Made in the USA
Middletown, DE
25 March 2024

52055404R00038